Battling Food Addiction

How to Maintain a Healthy and Fit Body while Getting Rid of High Carb Food

Introduction

I want to thank you and congratulate you for downloading the book, *"Battling Food Addiction."*

This book contains proven steps and strategies on how to overcome food addiction and establish a healthy relationship with food.

Have you ever felt like you cannot just stop eating? You know what you are repeatedly eating in large amounts is unhealthy, and it is not good for you but you cannot stop eating it. What is wrong with you, you may wonder? Are you out of your mind or are you just an in-disciplined person?

Well, if this describes you, you should know one thing. You are not a bad or an irresponsible person, not in a million years. What you are doing though, is that you have let food take over your life and you may be battling with addiction for food.

Food addiction is real, and it is quite common. In fact, according to foodaddictioninstitute.org/, about 20% of people considered to have a healthy weight, 30% of those who are overweight and 50% of people who are obese are addicted to a type of food, a combination of foods or specific volumes of food.

The question now is, can you overcome food addiction? The answer is yes. You can reclaim your health back from food addiction and maintain a healthy and fit body going forward. How?

The how is what this guide is going to discuss today. In this book, you will learn more about food addiction and the steps to overcome this addiction. By the end of this guide, you should be empowered to overcome your food addiction and have a healthy relationship with food because unlike other addictions that you have to abstain completely, you will still need to eat; hence, the importance of having a good relationship with food.

Thanks again for downloading this book, I hope you enjoy it!

© **Copyright 2019 - All rights reserved.**

This document is geared towards providing exact and reliable information in regards to the topic and issue covered. The publication is sold with the idea that the publisher is not required to render accounting, officially permitted or otherwise qualified services. If advice is necessary, legal or professional, a practiced individual in the profession should be ordered.

- From a Declaration of Principles which was accepted and approved equally by a Committee of the American Bar Association and a Committee of Publishers and Associations.

In no way is it legal to reproduce, duplicate, or transmit any part of this document in either electronic means or printed format. Recording of this publication is strictly prohibited and any storage of this document is not allowed unless with written permission from the publisher. All rights reserved.

The information provided herein is stated to be truthful and consistent, in that any liability, in terms of inattention or otherwise, by any usage or abuse of any policies, processes, or directions contained within is the sole and utter responsibility of the recipient reader. Under no circumstances will any legal responsibility or blame be held against the publisher for any reparation, damages, or monetary loss due to the information herein, either directly or indirectly.

Respective authors own all copyrights not held by the publisher.

The information herein is offered for informational purposes solely and is universal as so. The presentation of the information is without a contract or any guarantee assurance.

The trademarks that are used are without any consent, and the publication of the trademark is without permission or backing by the trademark owner. All trademarks and brands within this book are for clarifying purposes only and are owned by the owners themselves, not affiliated with this document.

Table of Contents

Food Addiction: An Overview 1
How Food Addiction Works 5
   Who is at a High Risk of Having Food Addiction 11
How to Overcome Food Addiction 13
   Understanding the Foods You are Addicted to 13
Lifestyle Changes to Overcome Food Addiction 17
   Step 1: Invest in Your Knowledge of Healthy Eating 17
   Step 2: Rewire Your Brain 19
   Step 3: Harm Reduction 20
   Step 4: Eat Three Meals Per Day 22
   Step 5: Eat the Right Portion of Food 23
   Step 5: Learn Healthy Coping Strategies 24
   Step 6: Join a Support Group 28
   Step 7: Exercising Regularly 29
Food Addiction Treatments 31
   Cognitive Behavioural Therapy 31

 12-Step Programs 32
 Medication... 32
 Commercial Treatments 33
 Nutritional Counselling 34
Conclusion 35

Food Addiction: An Overview

Food addiction is a behavioral addiction that is just like alcohol and drug addiction. When you are a food addict, your body becomes dependent on a particular type of food or eating behavior to the point that it needs that type of food to function properly.

Therefore, food addiction refers to when your need to eat becomes uncontrollable, and the best way to describe the feeling of being addicted to food is by studying your feelings when you are hungry.

When you go for an extended period without eating, what happens typically is you automatically start craving for food, and the more time it takes to get your next meal, the more your craving intensifies until it reaches a point where food becomes the most important thing in your mind. Now, that same feeling is what as a food addict, you continuously experience even when you have plenty of food to eat.

It is essential to mention that food addiction is much more intense than occasional binge eating. Food addiction is a strong obsession with food. This does not by any chance mean coming across an ice cream vendor and buying two ice creams, instead, it is the kind of obsession that makes you drive to a store in the middle of the night to get your favorite snack and doing that frequently without feeling that you are doing anything wrong.

Also, overeating that comes with food addiction is persistent. As a food addict, you constantly get the urge to overeat and as a result, you overeat almost every day. The funny thing though is when you are a food addict; you do not need to be hungry to overeat. You can overeat because of reasons that have nothing to do with hunger, and some of these reasons could include eating to cope with anger, stress or depression.

The interesting thing about food addiction is that you are not usually addicted to any food, for example, like vegetables. No, you are addicted to certain foods that are generally high in sugar and salt that activate the brain's reward system flooding your body with feel-good hormones once you take them (more on the reward system of your brain in the next chapter).

Below are some of the most highly addictive foods:

- Ice cream

- Pasta

- White bread

- Cookies

- Chocolate

- Candy

- Fries

- Cakes
- Juices that have additives
- Hot dogs
- Burgers
- High carbohydrate foods.

To understand food addiction, it is critical to comprehend your brain's reward system. We will look at this in-depth in the following chapter.

How Food Addiction Works

Your brain has a system called the reward system. This system's primary work is to reward your brain when you involve yourself in things that promote your survival like eating, spending time with loved ones, achieving a goal and engaging in physical intimacy.

So what does the reward system have to do with food addiction?

It has everything to do with food addiction. Here is why:

For starters, the part of the brain associated with drug addiction is also linked to the part of the brain related to food cravings and pleasure. More specifically, fast-digesting carbohydrates have been shown to stimulate brain regions involved in cravings and addiction. Studies show that desirable foods, like the ones mentioned in the previous chapter, trigger your pleasure center in the brain leading to a release in dopamine in large amounts.

When this occurs, you automatically feel good, and that feeling encourages you to repeat what you have just done to get that good feeling again and again or in other words, that 'high' you got.

Constant high-level of dopamine in your body automatically leads to two reactions. These two reactions are:

1. Tolerance

Because your level of dopamine is too high in your reward system, your brain adjusts to it by doing two things. One is reducing the dopamine receptors to reduce the ability of the cells you have in your reward circuit from responding to the hormone dopamine and two is the brain making less of the hormone dopamine. The brain does this to keep things balanced in your reward center.

When you have fewer receptors and low production of dopamine, what usually happens is you stop feeling that high you felt when you first consumed your favorite high carb food like ice cream. What this means for you is that to get that same level of high that you got from consuming an icecream, you will need to consume a higher quantity of ice cream. That process is what is called tolerance.

2. Withdrawal

When you have fewer dopamine receptors in your reward system, you will have little to no dopamine activity in your brain. What this will do to you is it will bombard you with feelings of sadness until you get your fix, which is eating what you are addicted to. This is what is called withdrawal.

The combination of tolerance and withdrawal is what encourages food addiction as you are caught up in a cycle where you need to eat more of a specific type of food to get a certain 'high' you got when you first ate that food. However, when you get it, it slowly fades away, making you experience withdrawal symptoms like feeling unhappy and sad, which forces you to go back to eating to improve your mood. That is how food addiction works.

How do you know you are a food addict and who is at a higher risk of being addicted to food? Move on to the next chapter to learn all that.

Are You a Food Addict?

When it comes to food addiction, you cannot take a blood or urine test to determine if you are an addict or not. However, below are some of the symptoms of food addiction that will tell you that you are probably addicted to food:

- Feeling guilty about consuming unhealthy food but repeating it soon despite the unpleasant feelings.

- Hiding from others when eating: This is mostly because your subconscious mind is telling you what you are consuming, which is unhealthy food, and the rate at which you are consuming it is wrong.

- Eating a particular food that you were craving and ending up overeating.

- You have obsessive food cravings for certain high carbohydrates foods.

- You need to eat for emotional release.

- Eating food, you crave to a point where you are excessively stuffed.

- Frequently making up excuses for your addiction: For instance, going to your friend's place and binging on chips and hot dogs and then telling yourself you only gave in to your cravings because it could have been rude to turn down your friend's food.

- Being unable to quit eating a particular type of food despite the physical problems that it causes: A good example is continuously eating sweets despite their negative impact on your dental health.

- Losing control over how much and where you eat craved food.

Those are the signs that show that you may be probably addicted to food. The thing about food addiction is that we have all at one point eaten more than we needed to, craved for food and gave in to the craving, and even reached for that comfort food to feel good; however, we have not all ended up addicted to food addiction. Therefore, who is really at risk of being a food addict?

Who is at a High Risk of Having Food Addiction

Below are some factors that can significantly increase your risk of developing a food addiction. These include:

- Being overexposed to highly palatable foods or foods, which creates a greater reward in your mind. Some of these foods are hot dogs, burgers, chips and most highly processed carb foods.

- Using food to cope with emotional stress over and over again until this is your default way of dealing with stress. For example, always reaching for ice cream, some cookies, potato chips, French fries each time you are having a bad day.

- Having genes that put you at a higher risk of developing food addiction: Studies in the recent past have shown increasing links between genes and eating patterns that have been associated with food addiction. For example, in the early 1990s, it was discovered that a group of obese study participants had the same dopamine gene market that was found in people addicted to alcohol and drugs. It was known as the "obesity gene"; however, it was later explained that obesity was simply a result of food addiction; hence, it was renamed as "food addiction gene."

With that understanding of food addiction, let us now move on to how to overcome food addiction and develop a great relationship with food.

How to Overcome Food Addiction

Overcoming food addiction has several phases, and we will go through those phases step-by-step. The first part is to understand your specific food addiction.

Understanding the Foods You are Addicted to

The first step to overcoming any addiction is acceptance. You need to come to the realization that binge eating on food even when you are full and then later feeling guilty about it is not normal eating behavior.

Once you accept that you have a problem, the next thing you need to do is to determine which food or foods are almost irresistible for you. Basically, what are your trigger foods?

This is important because just as a heroin addict's drug of choice is heroin, you also have a specific food or certain foods that you find it almost impossible to resist and if you have that food in the house, you have to eat it until you finish so that you can concentrate on something else. The question now is how do you know which food you are addicted to?

The best way to know which foods you are addicted to is to analyze your eating habits over a period. Look deep within yourself and try to figure out,

- Which food do you feel that you cannot live without?

- Which is that food type that you constantly think about, and you eat regularly?

Is it ice cream, cheesecake, burger, hot dog, candy, or chips? Take your time to think about it and come up with an accurate answer. Once you find your answer, you will need to test its authenticity by passing it through a couple of more questions. Remember, your goal here is to know precisely what you are addicted to, as that is the only way you can overcome your food addiction, and that's why it is essential to cross-check your answer.

Let us assume you found out your trigger food is a chocolate cake. Here are a few questions you can crosscheck your answer with:

1. Can you eat a chocolate cake long after you are full?

2. When you are stressed, anxious, or depressed, is chocolate cake the food you go to for comfort in dealing with those negative emotions?

3. Is chocolate cake worth waking up in the middle of the night?

4. Do you feel regret or guilt after you binge eat a chocolate cake?

5. Have you ever tried to stop eating chocolate cake, but for some reason, you have been unable to?

If your answer to all the above questions is yes, then chocolate cake is your "drug" of choice. If your answer to all the above questions is no, then chocolate cake is not your trigger food, which means you need to go back to the drawing board and come up with food or foods that pass most of those questions above. That said it is normal for you to find that you are addicted to two or even more foods.

Now that you know what you are addicted to, let us look at what options are at your disposal.

You have two options when it comes to overcoming food addiction. One is through food addiction treatments, and the other one is through following some simple lifestyle changes. Let us start by looking at lifestyle changes you can make to overcome food addiction.

Lifestyle Changes to Overcome Food Addiction

Here are some simple lifestyle changes that you can make on your own to overcome food addiction:

Step 1: Invest in Your Knowledge of Healthy Eating

As mentioned earlier, eating highly rewarding foods such as ice cream, cookies, French fries, burgers, sodas, etc., is something most of us have done, though this should be done occasionally. As mentioned previously, continually exposing yourself to these highly palatable foods then increases your chances of developing a food addiction. However, you also do not want to deprive yourself because this can easily lead to relapses. What then should you do?

The first thing you need to do is learn about healthy eating and start focussing on eating healthier balanced meals that are also tasty but will not have the same effect on your reward centers as the highly addicted foods.

You would also benefit significantly by learning how to make simple foods such as chicken and broccoli tasty so that you do not feel like you are missing out when you are not having your piece of cake or ice cream or those French fries, which will also ensure sustainability in the long-term.

Remember that food addiction is different from other addictions because with food addiction, you will still have access to the food, and you still need to eat; hence, the need to having a healthy relationship with food unlike other addictions such as addictions to drugs and substances where you have to abstain completely.

Step 2: Rewire Your Brain

You now know what you are supposed to eat, and so the next step for you is to rewire your brain to go back to how it was before you were addicted to certain foods.

Now the second step you need to take is to heal and rewire your brain back to the factory setting if we may call it that. So, how are you supposed to do that? There is only one answer, and that is by putting a stop to the cycle of tolerance and withdrawal. How can you do that? By simply eliminating the trigger food that you are addicted to.

Therefore, if you are addicted to ice cream, stop eating ice cream. If you are addicted to chocolate cake do the same. Whatever processed foods that you turn to and that fuel your addiction, stop eating it.

What this will do is that it will stop the process you were used to where your brain could release the feel-good hormone dopamine excessively because the high carb food you are eating is so rewarding, forcing your brain to reduce the dopamine receptors. Stopping this process helps your brain to heal and to detoxify; thus, enabling it to rewire and go back to how it operated before you got addicted.

A great way of ensuring you do this is for starters; stop buying those foods that you are addicted to. Also, as you get started, avoid eating out, as this exposes you to the foods you were addicted to, and makes it even harder.

Step 3: Harm Reduction

Just like any other addiction, putting a stop to something that you were addicted to is extremely tough. In fact, if we are honest, it can take a toll on your body as you will constantly get some withdrawal symptoms that might not necessarily be as lethal as the ones drug addicts and alcoholics get, but they will be devastating none the less. Some of these symptoms may include headaches, being moody, feeling unhappy and losing focus occasionally. Generally, your life will be less exciting.

That said, there is something you can do that can ease your transition of eliminating that food your body was used to, and that is doing some harm reduction as your third step towards overcoming food addiction.

Harm reduction is a process where you replace your unhealthy high carb foods with healthy, unprocessed food options that are slightly similar to the food you have just eliminated.

Below are suitable replacements for when craving for the mentioned unhealthy foods:

- Ice cream- you can substitute it with a cold fruit salad with some yogurt

- Chocolate- replace it with nuts

- Soda- substitute with fresh fruit juice

Finding suitable replacements for foods you love will make the whole process much easier

Step 4: Eat Three Meals Per Day

Now that you have eliminated the food you are addicted to, and you have replaced it with a healthy alternative, the next thing that you should do is to start eating three meals a day. Why is this important? Here is why:

When you stop eating a particular food that your body was used to, your body does not take that lying down. It fights back through giving you signals that come out as withdrawal symptoms like the ones I just mentioned. This is usually your mind's way of trying to twist your arm into relapsing, going back to unhealthy eating and eating the foods you were addicted to, and this mostly happens when you are hungry. Eating three meals a day helps you shut down your cravings by keeping your stomach full.

The other advantage of having a schedule where you eat three meals in a day is that it allows you to plan your meals; therefore, avoiding instances of opting for unhealthy food options.

Step 5: Eat the Right Portion of Food

Eating three healthy meals in a day is good for you when it comes to overcoming your food addiction. That said, for you to overcome your addiction and be able to live a healthy life and have a fit body, you will need to make sure that you eat the right portion of foods. How can you do that?

There is no one size fits all answer because we all have different energy outputs, weight, heights and other factors that affect the amount of food we need to eat to be healthy. What you need to focus on is eating until you are full and stopping to eat immediately; you feel full. To achieve this, you will need to be in tune with your body hunger and full signals, and to do that, you will need to practice mindfulness when eating.

Avoid eating when watching TV or being on your phone. When it is time to eat, focus on eating alone. Enjoy and savor each bite and start enjoying what you are eating. Avoid the need to gobble down and stuff yourself.

Step 5: Learn Healthy Coping Strategies

We were not born with food addiction. Basically, somewhere along the way, something changed that led you to be addicted to food. Therefore, the next step you must take is to take time to identify those social and environmental pressures that led you into over-eating and turning to food as your "drug" of choice.

This is important because you first need to make sure that you do not make the same mistake you made the first time of falling into a food addiction trap. Secondly, it is essential because the pressures that led you into food addiction are most likely still around and so you need to know how to deal with them to avoid relapsing.

How do you figure out what pressured you into an addiction?

Here are the questions you can ask yourself to figure out what caused your addiction.

1. What are the social pressures that always make me want to turn to food for comfort? Is it the numerous parties I go to frequently? Is it the many work meetings we have in the local cake shop? Or am I being influenced by the family gatherings I have? Take some time to figure out the social pressure that influences you and write it down.

2. What are the environmental pressures that make me want to binge-eat and forget myself? Is it the adverts that come on every so often on T.V when I am watching my favorite program? Or is it the pictures of cake and other delicious foods that I see in the magazines that I read? Find out the environmental pressures that influence you to eat and write them down.

3. What is usually my emotional state when overeating? Do I turn to food and forget myself when sad, angry, or annoyed or do I turn to food when I am happy and excited?

The above questions will jog your mind and help you come up with a list of triggers that lead you and can still lead you into addiction and then the next step will be to try and come up with a suitable way of dealing with those triggers when they come because they will arise. Let us assume the list below stands for your possible triggers.

- I always think about eating a chocolate cake

- I crave a chocolate cake when I pass by the cake shop which I do every morning as I go to work.

- I have a co-worker who always comes with a box of donut and sweet pastries, which has been really encouraging my addiction to cakes.

- I do not know what to know when stressed; therefore, I turn to food, specifically cake to feel better.

Now with that knowledge, come up with ways of how to deal with your possible triggers such as:

- I will find a new route to avoid the cake shop

- If I am hungry, I will snack on nuts instead; if not hungry, I will close my eyes and repeat these words, " Healthy food makes me feel good, unhealthy food makes me feel unenergetic when my co-worker is distributing snacks."

- When I am stressed or not in the best mood, I will take a walk or go to my happy place and think about something nice. I will also learn how to meditate to know how to deal with stress.

Step 6: Join a Support Group

According to research, you can stick with a positive change more if you have a support group. Transitioning from being a food addict to establishing a healthy relationship with food is not an easy task, especially if your eating behaviour is something that has been going on for years. However, having a support group usually eases this process because when you have people, you can talk to and share your experiences with overcoming your addition you get to feel much better by simply sharing and then secondly you get to receive encouragement and motivation that keeps you going.

Therefore, take some time to find a support group. You can do that by searching online to see if you can find a support group for food addicts or people struggling with eating disorders and join. If you cannot find any online, then you can opt to join an online forum.

You can also share with close friends and family members about your struggles and get support from them too. Basically, don't try to go it alone; you need accountability, and telling suitable people about your struggles keeps you accountable.

Step 7: Exercising Regularly

We all know that exercise is great for the body. However, here is something that you may not know, and that is exercising can help you overcome addiction. How, you may wonder? Here is how:

As you now know, when you are addicted to food, your mind and body craves for a specific type of food and in most cases, it is a high-carb food. This is mainly because most high-carb foods high in sugar and salt significant influence your reward centers in the brain, which then gives you a high. Now, did you know that exercising can also give you that high too? Well, if you did not know, now you know. When you exercise, your brain releases feel-good hormones, which makes you to feel great leading to what is commonly known as "runners high." This 'high' gives you a sense of accomplishment as well as increasing your confidence.

Therefore, exercising regularly helps you to get rid of food addiction by replacing the high you got from food addiction with the high you get with regular exercising.

The other good thing about exercising to overcome food addiction is that you also get other benefits that come with exercising like helping you to lose weight and sleeping better, which enables you to have a fit body and live a healthier life.

In addition to the above lifestyle changes to overcome food addiction, you can also opt for food addiction treatments. Let us look at that in the following chapter.

Food Addiction Treatments

This method consists of several programs and therapies that provide you with food addiction treatments. The thing about this method is that it is not a do it yourself approach; you will need to rely on professionals to help you deal with the addiction That said it is a very effective method and below are some of the food addiction treatments that have been found to work wonders when it comes to treating addiction.

Cognitive Behavioural Therapy

Cognitive behavioral therapy or CBT as many know it is a fantastic method when it comes to treating eating disorders. Over the years, it has had impressive results when dealing with eating disorders like bulimia.

12-Step Programs

One of the best ways you can use is by joining a 12-step program. A 12-step program is a group meeting where people with different addictions can come together, share about their addictions and even find a sponsor who can hold them accountable. The 12-step programs are usually free. Below are some worldwide 12-step programs that you can join.

- Food Addicts in Recovery Anonymous (FA)

- Overeaters Anonymous (OA)

- Greysheeters Anonymous (GSA)

Medication

The Food and Drug Administration (FDA) has not approved any medicines that can treat food addiction. However, one drug has been known to treat food addiction and it does it exemplary well. In Europe, it is called Mysimba and in the U.S is called Contrave. This drug t aids weight loss and has been proven to be very effective at curbing overeating. It curbs overeating by targeting some of the pathways in your brain that take part in the addictive nature of food and the good news is, the drug is approved by the Food and Drug Administration.

Commercial Treatments

Commercial treatments are programs that are similar to the 12-step programs you just learned a while ago. The only difference between them is that commercial treatment programs are not free. Here are a couple of commercial treatments programs that you can join:

- Bittens addiction situated in Sweden

- PROMIS which is based in the U.K

- COR Retreat which is based in the U.S

- ACORN which is based in the U.S

Nutritional Counselling

You can also opt for nutritional counseling. Nutritional counseling is beneficial as it enables you to develop a healthy approach to the food choices you make. It also helps you when it comes to meal planning. Basically, it gives you the knowledge to know what is healthy and what is not and that automatically enables you to start making healthier food choices little by little.

Conclusion

Thank you again for downloading this book!

I hope this book was able to help you to learn about food addiction and the steps you can take to overcome this addiction.

The next step is to actually take the first step and admit that you have a problem, remember that only the ones who apply this will get results so now you know what to do and now you can start working on making lifestyle changes to overcome the addiction. If you feel like you are not making any headway, don't hesitate to opt for the treatment options mentioned.

Thank you and good luck! On your journey towards this goals.

Printed in Poland
by Amazon Fulfillment
Poland Sp. z o.o., Wrocław

58648065R00028